12 THINGS TO KNOW ABOUT
THE STOCK MARKET

by Lois Sepahban

12 STORY LIBRARY

www.12StoryLibrary.com

12-Story Library is an imprint of Peterson Publishing Company and Press Room Editions.

Produced for 12-Story Library by Red Line Editorial

Photographs ©: Thinkstock, cover, 1, 13, 14, 16, 22, 29; Monkey Business Images/Shutterstock Images, 4; Robert Brown Stock/Shutterstock Images, 5; Richard Drew/AP Images, 6; Fuse/Thinkstock, 7; Shutterstock Images, 8, 9, 10, 15, 28; Peter Dejong/AP Images, 11; Mark Lennihan/AP Images, 12; Luis Louro/Shutterstock Images, 17; Andy Dean Photography/Shutterstock Images, 18; Bettmann/Corbis, 19; Peter Morgan/AP Images, 21; Andrey_Popov/Shutterstock Images, 23; Moreno Novello/Shutterstock Images, 24; Library of Congress, 25; AP Images, 26; Louis Lanzano/AP Images, 27

ISBN
978-1-63235-034-3 (hardcover)
978-1-63235-094-7 (paperback)
978-1-62143-075-9 (hosted ebook)

Library of Congress Control Number: 2014946812

Printed in the United States of America
Mankato, MN
October, 2014

Go beyond the book. Get free, up-to-date content on this topic at 12StoryLibrary.com.

TABLE OF CONTENTS

The Stock Market Is Not a Place 4

There Is More Than One Stock Exchange 6

Owning a Stock Is Owning a Piece of a Company 8

The First Stock Exchange Was Founded in 1602 10

The Stock Market's Purpose Is to Raise Money 12

Many People Work in the Stock Market 14

There Is No Set Price for Stocks 16

Stock Averages Show How Strong the Market Is 18

The Value of the Stock Market Always Changes 20

There Are No Guarantees in the Stock Market 22

The Stock Market Can Crash 24

Laws Make Sure the Stock Market Is Fair 26

Fact Sheet 28

Glossary 30

For More Information 31

Index 32

About the Author 32

THE STOCK MARKET IS NOT A PLACE

The stock market is a term that describes buying and selling stocks. It is not an actual place people can visit. People do not buy stocks at a stock market the same way they would buy an apple at a grocery store.

All of the stocks that are bought or sold in the world are part of a stock market. The stock market is global. People and

People across the world communicate to buy and sell stocks.

$55 trillion

Value of shares traded in the world stock market in 2013.

- The stock market is how we refer to the organized network of people who buy and sell shares in companies.
- It is not a place you can visit, such as a grocery store.
- It is not limited to one country or region.
- Companies that sell shares in the stock market need to raise money. Investors buy those shares and the company gets the money it needs.

SCRIPOPHILY

Companies issue paper certificates for their stock. Stock certificates show the number of shares that are owned by whoever has the certificate. Stock certificates, especially old ones, are popular with collectors. These old stock certificates are valuable even if the company no longer exists. The study and collection of stock certificates is called scripophily.

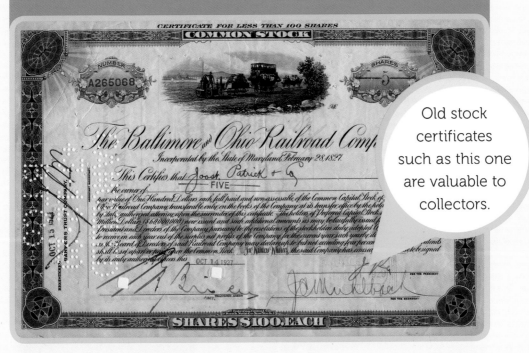

Old stock certificates such as this one are valuable to collectors.

companies all around the world can buy and sell stocks. An investor in Los Angeles can buy stock in a company in Beijing. An investor in Tokyo can buy stock in a company in London.

When a company needs money, one way to get that money is to sell stocks. Investors, or people who buy stock in a company, will give the company money. In return, the investors own part of the company. Companies that want to sell stock are listed on a stock exchange. The stock exchange is the actual place where investors can buy stocks.

THERE IS MORE THAN ONE STOCK EXCHANGE

Countries around the world participate in the stock market. Most of them have at least one stock exchange. In the United States, there are several main stock exchanges. The New York Stock Exchange (NYSE) is on Wall Street in New York City. The American Stock Exchange is now part of the NYSE. The National Association of Securities Dealers Automatic Quotation System (NASDAQ) is the largest electronic equities market in the country. Two other major exchanges are the Chicago Board of Operations and International Securities Exchange.

Different stock exchanges may sell different types of stocks. NASDAQ, for example, sells a lot of technology stocks. But that does not mean a technology company has to list its stock on NASDAQ. Companies choose where they want to list their stock. At the same time, stock exchanges can choose the

The floor of the New York Stock Exchange is a busy place.

companies they list. A company does not have to list its stock on a particular stock exchange. And a stock exchange does not have to list a particular company.

60
Number of stock exchanges worldwide listed on the World Federation of Exchanges.

- A stock exchange is a place where stocks are bought and sold.
- Companies can list their stocks on many different stock exchanges at the same time.
- Major stock exchanges in the United States include the NYSE, the American Stock Exchange, and NASDAQ.
- Foreign stock exchanges include the London Stock Exchange in England, the SIX Swiss Exchange in Switzerland, and the Zhengzhou Commodity Exchange in China.

OPEN OUTCRY VERSUS ELECTRONIC EXCHANGE

The traditional way stocks are bought or sold is called open outcry. Stock exchange workers who are buying or selling stocks of a company meet at a post on the stock exchange floor. There, they bid on the selling price of the stock. Today many stock exchanges use electronic exchange. In electronic exchange, bidding happens electronically. Advanced computer systems match up buyers and sellers.

Many technology companies choose to list their stock on NASDAQ.

OWNING A STOCK IS OWNING A PIECE OF A COMPANY

Some people put their extra money in savings accounts at their banks. Investors are people who put their extra money in stocks. When investors hold stock in a company, they own a piece of that company. Investors want to buy stocks at a low price and then sell them at a high price. If they can do that, they will make money.

Most investors research a company before they purchase its stock.

When investors are ready to buy stocks, they will look at the company listings on a stock exchange. Investors cannot go to the stock exchange and buy stocks. They have to buy or sell stocks through a broker. A broker is someone the government allows to buy or sell stocks at the stock exchange. Investors tell their brokers what they want to buy. The broker might make the sale online, over the phone, or in person. The way sales are made is different for each stock exchange.

The first step in trading stocks is bidding. A broker who is selling offers stock for sale at a certain price, for example, $20. Another broker offers to buy that stock for $15. A second broker might

Brokers bid against each other on stocks.

offer $16. The first broker might lower the asking price to $19. The brokers finally make a deal when the buying and selling numbers match.

700
Number of traders on the NYSE floor in May 2013.

- Owning stock is owning a piece of a company.
- The price of a stock can go up and down as people bid on it.
- Investors use brokers to purchase stocks.

THINK ABOUT IT

Investing in the stock market is one way to make money to put away for savings. Some people put most of their extra money in stocks. They might make money or lose money this way. Others prefer to keep their money in a savings account. Money there grows very slowly unless someone adds more money to the account. Which way would you save your money? Write at least two sentences explaining your choice.

4

THE FIRST STOCK EXCHANGE WAS FOUNDED IN 1602

Local stock markets have been around since the Middle Ages. Back then, moneylenders would meet in the market square. They would loan money to people or invest in local businesses. Over the years, some lenders did business in other towns. Some grew their businesses into other countries.

24

Number of investors who signed the Buttonwood Agreement to form the New York Stock Exchange on May 17, 1792.

- In Europe during the Middle Ages, brokers and lenders met in local marketplaces to make business deals.
- The Amsterdam Stock Exchange is considered the first organized stock exchange in the world.
- Following the Amsterdam Stock Exchange, stock exchanges were established in other places, including London, Philadelphia, New York, Brussels, and Mumbai.

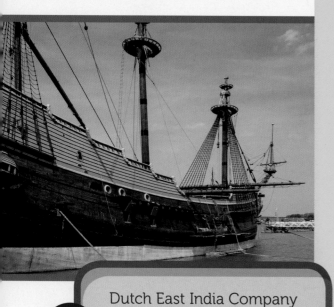

Dutch East India Company ships sailed between Europe and East Asia.

DAMRAK

The street most often associated with the stock market is Wall Street in New York. But nearly 200 years before Wall Street's stock exchange, another street was best known for stocks. That street was Damrak in Amsterdam. In 1602, the Amsterdam Stock Exchange was officially set up there. In 2000, it merged with two other European exchanges. They formed the Euronext Amsterdam. It is still found on Damrak Street.

The Euronext Amsterdam building on Damrak Street

But it was not until 1602 that an organized stock exchange was established. The Dutch East India Company shipped goods from the Far East to Europe. In order to expand, the company needed money. Beginning in 1602, the Dutch East India Company sold shares of its company to investors. It did so on the Amsterdam Stock Exchange.

The Amsterdam Stock Exchange was successful. Investors, brokers, and companies made a lot of money buying and selling stocks. Over the next 200 years, stock exchanges were set up in other places. London, Philadelphia, New York, and Brussels each had their own stock exchanges.

THE STOCK MARKET'S PURPOSE IS TO RAISE MONEY

Companies need money to do business. They need money for machines and equipment. They need to pay employees. They must purchase supplies. If a company does not have the money it needs, it may decide to sell shares to investors in the form of stock.

Before a company can sell its stock, it must become a private corporation. This allows the company to divide its shares among several private investors, called stockholders. After a period of time, the stockholders may decide to sell more of its shares to public investors. The first time a corporation starts selling shares publicly is called the

Banners fly at the NYSE during social media company Twitter's IPO.

@twitter

initial public offering, or IPO. In an IPO, the company sells its own stock. Investors who buy stock from the company can then sell it to other investors later. Because of this, stocks often have a low price during an IPO. If investors can buy stocks for a low price and then sell them for a high price, they will make a lot of money.

Wall Street has been the home of the NYSE since 1792.

1

Rank worldwide of the NYSE in IPOs in number and money raised in 2013.

- The purpose of the stock market is to raise money for corporations.
- The IPO is the first time a company sells shares on a stock exchange.
- Companies can sell shares.

WALL STREET

Wall Street in New York City is one of the most famous streets in the world. Today $55 trillion is traded in the global stock market there. The New York Stock Exchange was set up on Wall Street in 1792. Back then, Wall Street was just a dusty road. The first brokers met under a buttonwood tree at number 68 on Wall Street. Today's NYSE building is not far from the original site. More than 200 years later, it is still located on Wall Street.

13

MANY PEOPLE WORK IN THE STOCK MARKET

Many people work in the stock market. There are many different jobs to do. All these jobs help companies sell stocks and investors buy them.

A stock broker is the person who represents either a stock's buyer or its seller. Brokers pay fees to the stock exchange so they can buy or sell stocks there. These fees can be very high. The fee to buy and sell stocks at the NYSE is $40,000 for one year.

A market maker also buys and sells stocks. But where a broker buys and sells for an investor, a market maker

Stock brokers must pay to be able to trade stocks on the NYSE.

Analysts help brokers make good decisions about the stocks they buy and sell.

buys and sells stocks for itself. Market makers can be companies or individuals. They operate like investors. Their goal is to make money by buying stocks for a low price and selling them for a high price.

An analyst works at a brokerage house, just like a stock broker. Analysts, though, do not buy and sell stocks. Instead, they study companies. Then, they recommend which stocks a broker should buy or sell.

0.5 to 5

Amount, in cents, a broker working on the NYSE floor may make per sale of one share.

- There are many different jobs in the stock market.
- Brokers buy and sell stocks for investors.
- Analysts study companies to see where investors should buy or sell.

THINK ABOUT IT

What would it be like to work in the stock market? Pick one of the jobs described on these pages that you might like to do. Why does that job sound appealing? Write a paragraph explaining your answer using information from this book.

THERE IS NO SET PRICE FOR STOCKS

There is an old saying in the stock market: "A stock is worth only what someone is willing to pay." This is true. Investors may want to sell their stocks for $100 per share. But that does not mean they will. The highest bid for their stocks might only be $75 per share. If they do not want to sell their stocks for $75 per share, they can wait. Days, weeks, or years down the road, the price of their stocks might go up to $100 per share. Or it might not.

Buying and selling stocks is risky business. Free market forces decide

Stock prices go up and down over days, weeks, and even years.

how much a stock is worth. When investors talk about free market forces, they are really talking about supply and demand. Supply is how much of something there is. Demand is how many people want it.

There are many reasons people might want to own a part of a company. One reason is if they think its products are going to be successful. Apple announced the first iPhone on January 9, 2007. The phone was very popular. A year later on January 9, 2008, the price of Apple's stock had doubled to $179.40. The reason was that the product was exciting to people, and that made more people interested in the company.

$8,661
Average global value of a stock transaction in 2013.

- The free market forces of supply and demand determine stock prices.
- Investors can wait to sell stock to try to get a higher price.
- More demand for a stock may increase its price.
- Less demand may decrease a stock's price.

When stock is in demand, bidding can be exciting.

STOCK AVERAGES SHOW HOW STRONG THE MARKET IS

The stock market is not the only place to invest money. Investors might want to buy and sell real estate instead. Or they might want to buy and sell government bonds. Investors make decisions about where to put their money depending how well certain investments are doing. Sometimes real estate is the best place to invest. Other times the stock market is the best place to invest.

In 1896, Charles Dow wanted to show investors how strong the stock market was. He took 12 stocks. He added up their prices and then divided them by 12 to find

Some people choose to buy and sell real estate to make money.

30

Number of companies whose stocks are now compared on the Dow Jones Industrial Average.

- Dow Jones Industrial Average, S&P 500, and NASDAQ Composite Index calculate stock averages. Stock averages tell investors how well the stock market is doing.
- Charles Dow invented the first stock average.

the average price. He charted the averages over time. His charts and graphs showed trends in the price of stocks. These trends could be rising stock prices or falling stock prices.

Today investors use several stock averages. Some of the best-known are the Dow Jones Industrial Average, the S&P 500, and the NASDAQ Composite Index. Over the years, companies' shares have changed. Companies may split stocks or substitute one stock for another. Because of this, the averages use a special number to divide the total price of all the shares. These averages help investors decide if the stock market is the best place to put their money.

CHARLES DOW

Charles Dow created his stock average in 1896. At the time, the stock market was not popular with investors. The stock market seemed like a risky gamble. Dow wanted to show investors that the stock market was not as risky as they thought. He wanted to show investors they could make a good guess based on stock market trends.

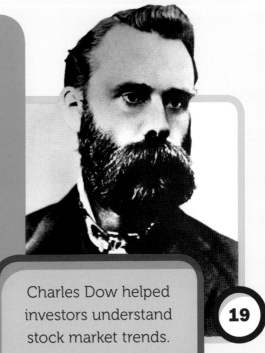

Charles Dow helped investors understand stock market trends.

THE VALUE OF THE STOCK MARKET ALWAYS CHANGES

Stock market averages show how stocks are doing over time. But on any given day, individual stock prices rise and fall. Sometimes stock prices change by just pennies. Other times stock prices rise and fall by much more.

These changes in stock prices are called market fluctuations. When the general trend of the stock market is rising prices, it is called a bull market. When the general trend of the stock market is falling prices, it is called a bear market. It is easiest to see these trends over long periods of time, like months or years.

Usually stock prices change slowly. There are times, though, when the

THINK ABOUT IT

Stock trends can be difficult to see day-to-day. It can be difficult to know when to buy or sell stocks. If you wanted to buy stocks, what tools would you use to choose when to buy? Use the information in this book to help you answer the question.

$500 billion

Amount lost on the Dow Jones Industrial Average on Black Monday.

- Market fluctuations are changes in the price of stocks.
- A bear market is when stock prices are falling.
- A bull market is when stock prices are rising.

The floor of the NYSE on Black Monday was a hectic place.

stock market makes big changes in one day. October 19, 1987, was one day like that. Today, it is remembered as Black Monday. On that day, the United States stock market lost 22.6 percent of its value. People sold stocks and bought other investments, such as bonds and gold. This caused a decrease in the price of the stocks. Imagine the value of the US stock market was $100 the morning of Black Monday. By the end of the day, the value had dropped to $77.40.

THERE ARE NO GUARANTEES IN THE STOCK MARKET

Those who invest in the stock market can make a lot of money. But they can lose a lot of money, too. There are no guarantees in the stock market. But there are possibilities. And everyone who participates in the stock market has the same goal: to make money.

The stock market offers benefits to companies and investors. When investors buy stocks, they have the chance to make money. At the same time, companies use the money from investors to grow or to run their day-to-day business. Sometimes investors do not have to wait to sell their shares in order to make money. Some companies pay the investor dividends. The amount of the dividend is based on how much

It is possible for investors to lose money on the stock market.

Some companies pay investors dividends throughout the year.

6,606

Number of corporations listed on NASDAQ, NYSE, and AMEX in September 2014.

- People invest in the stock market and companies sell stocks to make money.
- Investors can make a lot of money on the stock market, and companies get money they need to operate.
- However, there are no guarantees—investors can lose a lot of money on the stock market.

money the company has made. It also depends on how many shares an investor owns. Dividends are usually paid four times per year.

However, there are also some disadvantages to investing in the stock market. Buying and selling stocks is a gamble. No one knows for sure if they will make money. Sometimes, such as on Black Monday, stocks lose value before they can be sold. Sometimes companies lose money or go out of business. In those cases, investors lose.

THE STOCK MARKET CAN CRASH

When the stock market makes a big drop in a short period of time, it is called a crash. A crash is different from normal market changes.

Imagine a company sells three kinds of jackets: leather jackets, denim jackets, and nylon jackets. The leather jackets are the most popular. People buy them quickly. The denim jackets are less popular. The nylon jackets do not seem to sell at all.

The company decides to drop the price of the nylon jackets. It hopes this will make more people buy them. After a while, people are not buying denim or leather jackets

Supply and demand determines the prices of jackets—and stocks.

24

23

Percentage the average price of stocks fell on the Dow Jones Industrial Average on October 29, 1929.

- A stock market crash happens when the stock market drops sharply in a short period of time.
- The stock market crash of 1929 started the Great Depression.
- The stock market also crashed in 1987, 2000, and 2008.

Men in New York City wait in a line for food during the Great Depression.

THE GREAT DEPRESSION

In 1929, many Americans were living in debt. They bought items such as radios and cars on credit. If a car cost $1,000, they would pay $100 in order to take the car home. Then they would make payments every month to pay the other $900. In October 1929, the stock market crashed, creating a crisis. Companies went out of business. When that happened, people lost jobs. They could not pay their bills, such as payments toward their debt, or buy food. During the Great Depression, many families lost everything they owned. Many became homeless. In the United States, the Great Depression lasted until about 1940.

either. The company drops its prices on all of the jackets. But no one wants to buy them.

Next, a news program that says the coming winter is going to be much warmer than usual. People will not need to wear jackets to stay warm. Suddenly, everyone wants to get rid of their jackets. It does not matter how low the price of the jackets goes, no one will buy them. A similar scenario can happen with stocks. It can cause the stock market to crash. It means there are more sellers than buyers. The supply is greater than the demand. The value of stocks investors own drops, just like the price of jackets.

LAWS MAKE SURE THE STOCK MARKET IS FAIR

After the stock market crash in 1929, the United States government took action. It wanted to make sure that the stock market was fair for everyone. The Securities and Exchange Commission was formed.

The Securities and Exchange Commission, or SEC, is a government organization. In 1933 and 1934, Congress passed laws to set up the SEC. The job of the SEC is to protect investors and make sure the stock market in the United States is fair.

When people involved in the stock market break the law, it is called securities fraud. One kind of securities fraud is stock fraud. This happens when a broker lies to investors to get them to buy certain stocks. Another type of securities fraud is called insider trading. This happens when investors buy or sell certain stocks because they have secret information about a company.

A third type of securities fraud is called a Ponzi scheme or pyramid

The SEC headquarters in Washington, DC

Bernie Madoff ran the largest Ponzi scheme in history.

$20 billion

Amount investors lost in the largest Ponzi scheme in US history, run by Bernie Madoff.

- The purpose of the Securities and Exchange Commission is to protect investors.
- Securities fraud happens when investors are lied to in order to take advantage of the stock market. There are several types of securities fraud.
- In a Ponzi scheme, investors at the top are paid with money from scheme. In a legal business, investors earn money when the company pays dividends from what it has earned. But in a Ponzi scheme, the first investors in a new business are paid by the next investors. So the investors at the top of the pyramid make a lot of money. And the investors at the bottom of the pyramid lose a lot of money.

FACT SHEET

- The terms "stock market" and "stock exchange" are often used to mean the same thing. To be precise, though, it is important to remember that they are not the same thing. The stock market refers to the global market of buying and selling stocks. The stock exchange refers to the actual places where stocks are bought and sold. Some stock exchanges are physical places, while others are electronic. Brokers can buy and sell stocks over the phone and online.

- The terms "shares" and "stocks" are also often used to mean the same thing. There are slight differences between them, though. Both terms are used to mean ownership in a corporation. The difference is the way the terms are used. When investors talk about owning part of a specific corporation, they say they own shares in this company. When investors talk about owning part of corporations in general, they say they own stocks.

- The value of stocks, or how much they are worth, changes all the time. These changes can happen many times during the day. They are usually small changes. Sometimes, though, they can be sharp changes, causing the price to rise or drop by a lot. A share in a corporation can be worth $100 in the morning but only $75 in the evening. The share worth $100 is not the same as a $100 bill. The share might be worth $100 today. Tomorrow it might be worth $125. Two days from now, it might be worth $90. Investors who buy a share for $100 and then sell it for $125 have earned $25. But they could just as easily buy a share for $100 and watch its value drop to $50. If they sell it when it is only worth $50, then the investor lost $50. A $100 bill will still be a $100 bill two days from now, but $100 in stock might be worth more or less than that. The changing value of stocks is called market fluctuation.

GLOSSARY

bonds
Investments where the investor lends money to a company or government at a fixed interest rate.

corporation
A group that operates as if it is an individual in order to conduct business.

depression
A period of time when there is low economic activity and high unemployment.

dividends
Amounts of money a company gives investors.

fluctuations
Constant small changes.

free market
An economy based on unrestricted competition between different companies.

investments
Purchases that provide money for a business or property.

real estate
Land or buildings people purchase or invest in.

securities
Stock certificates, bond certificates, and other documents that prove ownership of an investment.

shares
Parts of a company an investor owns.

split
Dividing one stock share into multiple shares.

FOR MORE INFORMATION

Books

Blumenthal, Karen. *Six Days in October: The Stock Market Crash of 1929*. New York: Atheneum Books for Young Readers, 2002. Print.

Fuller, Donna Jo. *The Stock Market*. Minneapolis: Lerner, 2005. Print.

Orr, Tamra. *A Kid's Guide to Stock Market Investing*. Hockessin, DE: Mitchell Lane, 2009. Print.

Websites

The Mint: Fun for Kids
www.themint.org/kids/what-is-the-stock-market.html

The Stock Market Game
www.stockmarketgame.org/expstudent.html

The Wall Street Journal Market Watch: Virtual Stock Exchange Games for Kids
www.marketwatch.com/game/for-kids

INDEX

American Stock
    Exchange, 6, 7
Amsterdam Stock
    Exchange, 10, 11
analysts, 15

bear market, 20
Black Monday, 20, 21,
    23
bull market, 20
Buttonwood Agreement,
    10

Chicago Board of
    Operations, 6
crash, 24–25, 26

demand, 17, 25
Dow, Charles, 18–19
Dow Jones Industrial
    Average, 19, 20, 24
Dutch East India
    Company, 11

initial public offering
    (IPO), 12–13
International Securities
    Exchange, 6

Madoff, Bernie, 27
market fluctuations, 20,
    21, 29
market makers, 14–15

National Association of
    Securities Dealers
    Automatic Quotation
    System (NASDAQ), 6,
    7, 19, 23
New York Stock
    Exchange (NYSE), 6,
    7, 9, 10, 13, 14, 15,
    23

scripophily, 5
Securities and Exchange
    Commission (SEC),
    26, 27
securities fraud, 26, 27
stock averages, 18–19,
    20
stock brokers, 8, 9, 10,
    11, 13, 14, 15, 26,
    28
stock exchange
    (definition of), 5, 28
stock market (definition
    of), 4, 28
supply, 17, 25

Wall Street, 6, 11, 13

About the Author

Lois Sepahban has written several books for children, including science and history, biography, and fiction. She lives in Kentucky with her husband and two children.